LOST IN YELLOWSTONE

THE EXTRAORDINARY TRUE ADVENTURE
STORY OF TRUMAN EVERTS AND HIS
COURAGE, ENDURANCE AND SURVIVAL IN
THE WILDERNESS OF YELLOWSTONE
NATIONAL PARK

DRAKE QUINN

Copyright © 2019 by Drake Quinn.

Based on the story of Truman Everts.

All rights reserved.

No part of this book may be reproduced in any form or by any electronic or mechanical means, including information storage and retrieval systems, without written permission from the author, except for the use of brief quotations in a book review.

Dedicated to the memory of Truman Everts

INTRODUCTION

The story of Truman Everts survival for 37 days in Yellowstone is an astonishing tale of one man's struggle against the wilderness.

The year was 1870 and Truman was in his mid-50's. He'd been appointed by Abraham Lincoln to his post as Assessor for Internal Revenue in Montana, but his name would go down in history for some quite different achievement.

What started out as an expedition to explore the beauty of Yellowstone, soon turned into a fight for survival when he became separated from his companions.

When his horse bolted, Truman was left without guns or the most basic of supplies.

He tells the story in his own words, speaking of his

INTRODUCTION

battle with loneliness, his quest for fire and his struggles with the elements, as winter closed in around him.

He faces battles for his very life, when confronted by a mountain lion.

When he was finally found, Truman weighed less than 100 pounds. If ever a man was pushed to the very limits of human endurance, Truman Everts was that man.

150 years after these events took place, this extraordinary story of courage and endurance is one that continues to inspire and amaze today.

ONE
LOST IN YELLOWSTONE

My name is Truman Everts. Before we get started, I must warn you that Lost in Yellowstone is a true story. It happened to me, just as I am about to tell it to you.

I'd heard stories about the beauty of the Rocky Mountains while living in Montana. I'd listened to strange tales of the Yellowstone.

I began to imagine that participating in an Expedition to Yellowstone would be both interesting and worthwhile.

I supposed that the hardships of traveling by horseback through the rough terrain would be well rewarded by the grandeur of the natural scenery, of which I'd heard tell.

Of course, the thought of getting utterly lost, without

food; the concept of wandering for days in the wilderness, was something I had not once considered.

Some days into our expedition, I became separated from my companions. Our way was blocked by a dense pine forest, fallen trees, which made progress almost impossible.

As I tried to make my way past one of these enormous trees laying prostrate on the forest floor, I happened to stray out of sight and hearing of my companions.

It had been a busy day, and it was late in the afternoon. I was tired, and perhaps it was for this reason that becoming separated from my friends didn't give me any cause to worry. I rode onwards, confident that I'd soon be rejoining my friends and sharing the story around the campfire.

I rode on until darkness made traveling through the dense forest too dangerous. To have no sustenance for the evening was indeed disagreeable, but I smiled to myself as I imagined telling the story to my friends around the campfire.

On the following day, I rose at dawn, mounted my horse and rode in what I felt sure was the direction of our camp. I could picture my friends camping on the lake shore, awaiting my arrival.

The falling pine needles had obliterated any trace of the trail for which I was searching. The best I could do was to examine the ground in vain for tracks or indications that my companions had traveled this way.

I came to a clearing in the forest where there were several ways forward. I dismounted my horse, intending to choose which track which would lead me in the direction of my companions. I took a few paces into the forest.

As I was searching the ground for tracks, my horse took fright, and I turned around, to see him disappearing at full tilt through the forest. That was the last time I saw him.

Everything, except the clothing I stood up in, my opera glasses and a couple of knives, had been attached to the horse's saddle - my blankets, gun, matches and fishing tackle had all vanished with my horse.

Even so, I was not anxious. The thought that I could be permanently separated from my companions was not something which I had entertained. Instead, I spent my efforts on trying to track down the horse, albeit in vain.

Realizing that I was indeed separated from my companions, I wrote some notes for them and posted them along my route, in case they should pass this way.

After this, I struck out into the forest, heading in the direction of their camp. As the day passed, I began to feel alarmed at the thought of spending another night alone, without either food or fire.

Yet, I continued to hope that I would soon come across my friends and we would all soon be laughing at my strange adventure.

As I pressed on, I began to realize that I could be in real danger. I sat down on a log, trying to figure out my next step.

As best as I could guess, my companions must have passed close to the spot where I had placed the notices and would now be waiting for me to rejoin them. As darkness was falling, I realised that I must spend yet another night alone, before rejoining them.

I spent the night on a bed of pine needles, in the pitch dark, now more aware than ever of the danger I was in. As I looked upwards through the tree branches, the wind sighed through the pine, and the forest was alive with the barking of coyotes and the long howl of the gray wolf. These same sounds had accompanied us many nights on our travel thus far, but tonight they filled me with terror. Sleep came fitfully.

I awoke and pushed forward to the place where I had posted my notice. No-one had passed this way. I sat down, overwhelmed with disappointment. For the first time, the realization came over me that I was lost.

Not only lost, but lost without food or means to make a fire. I was alone in the wilderness, over a hundred miles from human habitation and surrounded by wild animals.

To stop myself from becoming despondent, I resolved in my mind, "not to perish in the wilderness."

I still hoped that I would be able to rejoin my party, if I could only find the location of their camp.

I rose from my seat and pushed my way through the thick forest branches. A feeling of physical weakness replaced hunger.

From time to time, as I scrambled over a fallen tree or pushed through a thicket, a sense of exhaustion would come over me. Each time I felt like sinking, I'd say out loud, "I simply must find my friends."

In my worst imaginings, I'd think of my daughter, and how news of my starvation or terrible death might reach her.

At this time, a recent debate was brought to mind, in

which we had discussed whether each man had within him the self-preservation skills necessary to rise to any emergency. This spurred me on, as I felt that it must indeed be so.

I now record this thought, so that anyone who might read this, if you ever find yourself in a similar situation, may not succumb to despair, however desperate it might at first seem. Such a thought can give life to hope, stem hunger and revive the spirit.

It was noon when I stepped out of the forest into an open space. My surroundings were undeniably magnificent, with the lake before me glittering in the sunlight.

As I approached the sand at the lakeshore, I observed that rising above me was the loftiest peak of mountains, that appeared never-ending. The sparkling jet of a geyser, with the rising mists from the many hot springs, made this one of the most impressive landscapes I had ever seen.

Never before had I seen so much wildlife - mink and beaver swam around me unafraid; deer and elk looked at me in a surprised fashion and otters swam in and out of the water with astounding agility.

In any other circumstances, this scene would have transfixed me with amazement; yet, tired, anxious and hungry, I struggled to take it all in or even appreciate the fact that I was probably the first man to behold this incredible sight. Instead, I longed only for the comfort of friends, food and a shelter over my head.

On the second day by the lake, while gazing out at the vast expanse of water, I spotted a canoe, with a single oarsman at the helm.

It was moving towards me fast. I rose and hastened to the beach, encouraged that, whoever it was, I would soon have food and be restored to my friends.

As I drew closer, it turned northwards, and the object of my hope turned out to be a large pelican, which flapped its wings and flew further up the shore.

This small incident completely demoralized me. In one moment, my joy turned to significant loss and a new awareness of the horror of my situation.

Even so, I knew darkness was approaching, so I began to look for a spot to rest for the night. As I did so, I found a small thistle-like plant, which seemed strange amongst the pines. Pulling it up by the root, it looked somewhat like a radish. I bit into it; it was palatable and nourishing. And so, I feasted on thistle root, it was my first meal in four days.

Eureka! At last, I had found food. With food, I realized that I could manage until I was able to find my friends once again. What a contrast to the misery of the past hour, and the disappearing canoe!

With hunger held at bay, I lay down beneath a tree, its many branches stretching out above me and fell asleep.

I have no idea how long I slept for, but I was woken suddenly by a loud scream, something like a human being in pain.

I knew that sound. I had heard it many times. It was the screech of a mountain lion, and it was alarmingly nearby.

For a moment every nerve in my body froze in terror. Then my instincts kicked in and I was rapidly ascending the branches of the tree, shouting back down towards the ground. I quickly rose among the branches until I was as high as I could safely climb.

Below me, I could hear the animal snuffling and prowling, on the exact spot on which I had been sleeping just moments before.

Each time the mountain lion roared, I would respond with a loud scream.

To try and alarm the lion, I broke off branches, hurling them down towards it. The lion continued circling the tree, roaring and lashing the ground with his tail.

My attempts to frighten it off had failed. I resigned myself to my fate. At that moment, I realized that I had not tried silence. Holding fast to the tree trunk, I stayed perfectly still.

Below me, the snuffling and prowling continued, though the silence was ever more terrible, as I waited for the lion to pounce.

Minutes passed like hours. I have no concept how long the lion prowled beneath me. At last, with a bound, it ran off into the forest. I was alive!

If I'd had the strength, I would have stayed aloft the tree until morning, but my ordeal had left me much weakened and I descended its limbs slowly. I lay down on the forest floor, where only recently the beast had been prowling and fell into a deep sleep.

When I awoke, all that had happened the night before seemed like a terrible nightmare, only the broken branches around me were testament to the reality of my experience.

Once again my thoughts turned to home, and my loved ones who might never have known my terrible fate, had I perished that night.

As I pondered this, an easterly wind brought a storm of snow, mixed with rain (the sort that happens at high altitudes) which set in. My clothing, torn as it was from the undergrowth, left me exposed to the elements.

I knew from experience that this storm would not blow over quickly. The hope of finding my friends now gone, I knew with certainty that if I were to escape this wilderness, it would have to be from my own efforts.

I realized that my situation was grave and that I must act, and quickly. Spreading the branches of a spruce tree over me, pulling over earth and branches for warmth. I lay there for two days, while the storm raged about me.

Only one thing transpired during those dismal days - a cold bird, hopped within arm's reach - starved and hungry, I grabbed it and killed it, devouring it raw.

On the third day, the storm abated and I made my path towards the hot springs in the shadow of the mountain.

I was chilled to the bone, my clothing wet through. I lay down next to a tree, the ground warm beneath me from the hot springs. Once the warmth started to permeate my body, I staved my hunger with a snack of thistle-roots.

Nearby I built a shelter of pine branches and hid here until the storm blew over. Thistles were plentiful here, and I felt they could sustain me, for the moment.

I stayed here for seven days, the first three of which the storm continued to rage and blow around me. Meanwhile, the vapor from the hot springs enveloped me, as if I was in a warm bath.

Hidden away here, all I could do was eat, sleep and think. My thoughts were given over to how best I could escape from this wilderness.

The want of fire was what most concerned me. I recalled everything I'd read about the making of fire, but to no avail. I knew that without the ability to make fire, escape from the wilderness was impossible. I'd either be attacked by wild beasts or perish in another storm, like the one which had just passed. It was only the warmth of the hot springs which had saved me on this occasion.

A thick layer of snow had fallen, and I hid in my pine branch refuge until it disappeared. As I lay there, I dreamt of creating some memorial, so that one day a passerby might know what became of me.

A ray of sunlight lit up the lake with sparkles, and with it, an idea came to my mind. There was a lens in my opera glasses, by which I could procure fire.

I immediately fell upon the task - imagine my joy

when I saw the beauty of smoke curling from the dry wood I held between my fingers.

At that moment I felt that, if the whole world were offered in exchange, I would deny it all, before parting with that precious spark.

I now had both food and fire, though the food was barely sufficient, yet with a fire now kindled, my hunger was momentarily forgotten.

In an unhappy accident, I managed to scald my hip which, added to my frostbitten feet, made movement harder and caused delays.

I had mislaid both my knives, so I managed to fashion a replacement by sharpening a buckle. With this, I managed to fashion some footwear, held together by strips of bark. Unraveling my handkerchief, I was able to mend my clothes. From the same material, I formed a fishing line, which attached to a pin, fashioned as a fish-hook.

On the morning of the eighth day of my arrival at the hot springs, I ventured forth on the next step of my journey.

The morning was beautiful, the sun was warm, and the air was fresh. For a moment, I felt exhilaration, that is until I felt once more my utter aloneness and separation from my companions.

From this day on, the days without food began to take a toll on me. It felt as if my mind was in a dreamland and I had strange imaginings.

The wind changed, and the sky clouded over, bringing colder air and the need for a warm fire. I pulled out my glass lens, but alas, there was no sun to shine. I sat down, waiting for a shaft of sunlight to break through, but night came, and the freezing cold found me on a bleak hillside, half-starved and barely clothed.

I believe that I only survived the long and terrible night by pacing up and down, rubbing my numb hands and feet against a log. Frozen, I retraced my steps to the lakeside, building my first fire by the beach and recovering there for a further two days.

If there had been the slimmest hope that my friends might search for me and find me, this now left me altogether. I knew that it was by my own exertions that I would have to escape.

I sat to plan my escape from the wilderness. I had a choice of three routes. One was to follow Snake River for about a hundred miles; another to cross the country by scaling the Madison Mountains; and the other, was to retrace my journey by which I had come to this place.

The last of these was the least inviting, as I was so familiar with the difficulties I would face.

I'd heard that the waters of the Snake River were hazardous, so dared not choose that route.

This left me with one choice, to travel across the Madison range, which seemed the shortest, yet proved to be a most unwise decision, as you shall see shortly.

I filled my pockets with thistle-roots and started for Yellowstone Lake. I stopped at noon to make fire, while the sun was highest in the sky and kept a small brand burning through regular blowing.

That night I lit a fire amid a dense thicket of pines. Around me, I could hear the screaming of night-birds, the Mountain lion and the wolves howling.

I sat with my back against a tree, the smoke from the fire enveloping me.

As I half sat, half lay there, I imagined blazing eyes in the thick forest; I fancied a pack of wolves ready to pounce on me in the darkness. I slept fitfully, longing for morning to come.

At dawn, I resumed my journey towards the lake. Sunset found me at a headland with a magnificent view of the mountains and valley - the peaks of the three Tetons rose in the distance. To my right, the

Madison mountains with their ravines, canons, and gorges glittered in the sunlight.

As I looked out at the magnificent panorama before me, I nearly forgot to make the most of the rays of the sun, to get a small firebrand burning.

Holding the brand in my hand, I descended to the beach of the lake. I kindled a fire and, kicking off my hand-fashioned shoes, walked barefoot along the soft, warm sand, gathering wood for the fire.

As dusk fell, I looked around for my slippers. One was found, but the other was missing. There was no option but to search for it, combing the hill-side and beach. After an hour my search was rewarded with the joyous discovery of the missing slipper.

Finally, I was able to rest - sitting on the sand and listening to the wild lullaby of the roaring waves.

After a refreshing sleep, I woke, stirred the remaining embers into flame and ate a cheery breakfast.

I resumed my journey, walking along the lakeshore - finding at noon, the camp where my friends stayed.

I found a dinner fork, which I pressed into service for digging roots and a yeast-powder can, which became my drinking cup. Though I look around for food, I found none (though I later discovered that they had indeed hidden some closer to where I had initially strayed from the camp). Dejected by this disappointment, I retraced my steps along the beach.

A spot of sunshine in the afternoon, allowed me to light a firebrand, which I carried to my camping place to build a fire. The wind had picked up, so making a shelter of pine branches, I crawled under it and was soon asleep.

I have no idea how long I slept there - but the sound of snapping, crackling and hissing woke me.

Both my shelter of branches and the nearby forest were on fire. My left hand was severely burned, and the fire had singed my hair back, as I escaped this ring of fire. In my hasty escape, I lost my buckle-tongue knife, my pin fish-hook, and tape fishing line.

The pine forest was soon a vast sheet of flame, the flames shooting hundreds of feet into the night sky, lighting up the lake and mountains around me. It was both terrible and full of grandeur. The sound of burning and falling branches was deafening, the air filled with acrid smoke. On and on it burned, until it felt as if the entire hillside was afire.

When the fire passed, all that remained was a blackened trail of devastation.

I could no longer search for a trail, so resolved to aim for the lowest part of the Madison range. For many hours, I made my way over the rugged hills, through fallen trees and thorny thickets.

The mountains mocked me, receding into the distance as I advanced.

I had taken the precaution of obtaining fire, so slept in warmth that night. The idea of finding a hidden pass into the Madison filled me with hope.

As I came closer, all I could see were endless peaks and precipices, rising thousands of feet sheer above the plain. There was no hidden gully or pass to help me through. Despair overwhelmed me. The last two days had been wasted; it was all in vain.

My only option now seemed to be down the Yellowstone. I felt strong enough to spend one more day searching for a pass. I had presumed that the thistles would be growing everywhere, so my supply was already gone. I searched the hillside in vain for them.

I needed to decide whether to search for a way through the Montana range or return to the Yellowstone.

It was at this time that I experienced the most strange hallucination. An old friend, whose wisdom I had always valued, appeared before me.

"Go back immediately, as rapidly as your strength

permits. There is no food here, and the idea of scaling these rocks is madness."

"Doctor," I replied. "It's too far; I cannot make it."

"Your life depends on it. Return at once my friend; it is your only chance," he urged. "Travel as fast as you can."

But Doctor," I replied, "My companions are just a few miles away. My strength is almost gone, my shoes are worn out, and my clothes are in tatters. I will climb this mountain or die trying."

"Don't even think of it. I will accompany you. Help yourself, and God will help you."

Persuaded at last and thrilled to have the Doctor as my traveling companion, I returned whence I had come.

After walking a few miles, I kindled a fire and slept peacefully.

As I started out the following morning, the sun was rising. From time to time, I would question the wisdom of taking this route, and as I did so, my old friend the Doctor would appear to offer some words of encouragement.

In the high altitudes of the mountains, distance is deceptive. After walking for two days, my destination seemed as far away as it had when I had set out.

On the afternoon of the fourth day, I kindled a fire and gathered some roots - they were the first thing I'd eaten in five days. As I lay down that night, I felt that my hopes of escape were slipping from my grasp.

At dawn, I started down the trail. My motto, "I will not perish in this wilderness," often came to mind and revived my spirits a little.

As I struggled through a mass of tangled trees which seemed never-ending, I paused to seriously consider whether it might be better to stop and die quietly here, than to pursue my plan of escape. The idea of escape seemed only to prolong my suffering.

A voice seemed to whisper to me across the wind, "While there is life, there is hope. Take courage." My thoughts thus disrupted, I rose and carried on.

I came to a clearing and found the fresh tip of a gull's wing. At once I kindled a fire, ground the wing to a powder, and made a broth of sorts, which I consumed with relish. At once I fell into a deep sleep.

I had reached the point where I no longer felt hungry; such was my starvation. Indeed, time itself seemed to be unimportant. Days and nights came and went. My mind wandered.

As I slept my dreams took me to fabulous restaurants in New York and Washington. I would sit down to enormous feasts and delicious dainties, and I imagined myself eating these delights until I was replete. Alas! The feasts were only in my dreams.

I arrived at the falls on a cold day, when the wind was moaning through the pines. The scene which had so captivated me only weeks before held no interest for me.

I waited in vain for a single ray of sunshine, with which to kindle a fire. But the sun remained hidden. There would be no fire that night.

I set about building a shelter of brushwood, with fallen leaves as my bed. Though I tried to sleep, the cold permeated my body, and it was only by rubbing my hands together and beating my legs that I did not freeze in my shelter that night.

When I rose the next morning, I was practically paralyzed with cold. I managed to make my way to the river and sat waiting for the sun to make its appearance.

Nothing in the majestic surroundings compared to the beauty of the sun coming out from behind the clouds and shining down on my glass lens. I kindled a flame, which I fed with every stick and branch I could gather and sat by it, warming myself through for several hours.

Just a short distance away the Yellowstone falls roared, but they had lost all their charm for me.

The Doctor who had been present with me until this point, now left me and was not seen again.

One day, I came across a stream, filled with small fish. I plunged my hands into the water, grabbed a handful and devoured them raw. This was a feast!

My stomach disagreed, and I found myself very sick indeed. I was thankful that I had not eaten more, as had been my desire. If I had done so, there's little doubt that I would have died, alone in the wilderness, in excruciating torment.

My mind wandered to the dark waters of despair, and I would long for the release of death. Then I would recall all that had happened on my journey - the incident with the mountain lion, the blazing forest fire and my return from the Madison ranges, at the request of the doctor. In all of these, I could sense mysterious protection. Where was my mysterious protector now, when I needed a little faith to take me onwards?

I thought of my daughter and longed to be restored to her, even if only for an hour.

Along the streams, I would often sit and try to catch a trout, using a hook that I had fashioned from my broken spectacles. I never had success.

If only I had my gun, there was game aplenty around me - I saw herds of antelope, elk, deer; I saw flocks of geese, ducks, and pelicans; even the occasional bear. I had no way to kill them, so I found their presence irksome.

One afternoon, I came upon a large hollow tree, near "Tower Falls." The many tracks around it gave me to believe that it was a bear's den. The inside looked most inviting as a place to rest.

Accordingly, I gathered wood and twigs, lit a circle of fires around the tree and climbed into the hollow tree for the night. When I awoke, I saw that the flames had burnt a large area of the nearby forest, which had doubtless saved me from the rightful owner of the den and any further adventures.

Arriving at "Tower Falls" I once again tried in vain to hook myself a trout. I tried to capture a grasshopper and finally determined that I would eat only thistles from this point onwards.

I left "Tower Falls" and entered the open country. The forest gave way to a desolate landscape, with only the occasional clump of dwarf trees.

I made camp that night and woke to find wind and

snowstorm had nearly extinguished my fire. With everything white with snow, I entirely lost my bearings. My only option was to find the river again and follow the direction of it's current.

Once I came to the edge of the canyon, below which lay the river, with great difficulty, I made my way down its rocky face. I drank with gusto from the pure waters and sat there for a while, hoping that the storm would soon pass, so that I could kindle a fire.

As the hours passed, it became clear that the sun would not be blessing me with an appearance. Chilled to the bone and soaked through, I scrambled up the canyon walls. It was hard work, and it was dark by the time I returned to my fire, which had nearly been blown out by the raging storm.

I lay two nights beside the fire, while the storm blew around me. Every night I would gather wood, brush and broken branches. I would snatch sleep in between these endeavours, and so I got little rest.

By this time, my arms had shrunk and were so thin that a small child could easily have put their hand right around them. "Yet," I told myself, "It is death to remain. I cannot perish in this wilderness."

As the sun rose, the snow rapidly melted and I continued my journey. Before leaving the forest, I had filled my pockets with thistles, knowing I was unlikely to find them in the open country beyond. As such, I had to ration myself, according to the number of days it would take me to reach civilization.

Two or three days before I was found, while climbing a steep slope, I collapsed from exhaustion into a bush. Without the energy to get up, I unbuckled my belt and fell asleep there.

When I woke, I fastened my belt and rose, continuing my course. Alas! When night fell, I gathered some brush for a fire and felt for my lens to kindle a flame. It was gone. If the earth had opened up to swallow me alive, I could not have been more alarmed. Without it, I was a dead man.

I lay down, overwhelmed with torment at my situation. My battle to escape the wilderness was over. As I lay there, the events of my life came before me, as in a dream.

After a while, my terror left me, and I came to myself. Thinking back I realized that I must have mislaid my glass when I had fallen asleep in the bush. There was only one course of action; I must retrace my steps to retrieve it. Imagine the joy and relief with which I found my lens in that exact spot.

Returning to my camp, I lit the brushwood, and lay down to rest. It began to snow, to keep the fire alive became principal purpose. I got no sleep that night.

The storm was still raging when I awoke, but I knew I must go on, in spite of it. Picking up a brand from the fire, I recommenced my journey.

After midday, the storm died down, and the sun made an appearance. Finding a small group of trees, I went about making my camp for the night; collecting wood and brush, together with some dry twigs, setting the brand down while I did so. In those short minutes, the brand expired, and though I blew on it to revive it, it was too late. It was late in the afternoon, and the sun was behind the clouds, I feared another freezing night without fire.

I sat there, holding my lens, waiting to catch a ray of sunlight. It felt as if my very life depended on it.

After a few moments, the clouds moved on, and the sun shone down. With trembling hands I held my lens as steadily as I could, anxious in case another cloud should obscure the sunlight. My patience was rewarded with a small plume of smoke, making its way heavenwards. Shortly after, the spark became a flame which warmed me all through that night.

In the morning, I continued my way onwards. By now, I was sure I should no longer rely on the sun for warmth, but carry a brand with me, or die.

I walked for a fair distance, but then the storm came on, and I was chilled to the bone. I tried to kindle a fire, but could not make it burn well. Picking up a brand, I stumbled on, convinced that the end was near. I had done everything humanly possible to escape the wilderness, but I knew that I was days away from death.

As I was now on the trail, there was some small relief in knowing that my remains would one day be found and the mystery of my fate ended.

Even then, I heard a small voice seem to whisper, "struggle on."

As I groped along the hillside, I became aware of a reflection. Looking upwards, two faces met my gaze.

"Are you Mr. Everts?"

"Yes. All that is left of him."

"We have come for you."

"Who sent you?"

"Judge Lawrence and other friends."

"God bless him and them and you! I am saved!" And with these words, after 37 days in the wilderness, I fell into their arms falling into a state of unconsciousness.

Baronet and Prichette made camp at that very spot. One left to get help from Fort Ellis, some seventy miles hence, the other waited with me, and took care of me.

Within two days, I was strong enough to be moved some miles down the trail to a miner's cabin.

I rested in a proper bed, a game broth was made, and the miners abandoned their work to help restore me to health.

The night after I arrived at the cabin I was suffering the deepest agonies. I feared that I had been saved from the wilderness, only to die amongst friends.

As I lay there, there came a knock at the cabin door and an old hunter entered. I told him my story, but when I told him of the agonies I was suffering, he at last spoke.

"Why, God bless you, there is a simple remedy for that. Wait here and I will bring it to you within two hours."

He returned with a sack, and proceeded to render down some bear fat, from the bear he had killed just a few hours earlier.

"Drink this," he said, and so I down about a pint of bear fat. The following day all my pain had gone and my appetite returned.

Soon I was well enough to leave the cabin and travelled to Bozeman, where I met my friends who kept me company until my health was fully restored and I could return home to my daughter.

I am thankful to the members of my Expedition, who spent days searching for me. I am thankful to Judge Lawrence who made the offer of a reward, which brought Baronet and Prichette to my rescue.

My story ends here, but I believe that the day is not far distant when the wonders and grandeur of Yellowstone will be accessible to all who love nature.

I myself long to return to behold the spectacular sights of Yellowstone once more, and to experience their power to delight and transport the mind with their majesty and wonder.

ONE MORE THING

If you've enjoyed reading or listening to this book, please consider leaving a rating or review. Thank you!

ABOUT THE AUTHOR

Drake Quinn is the author of *Campfire Stories for Kids*, a collection of spooky, fun and joke stories to tell around the camp fire.

www.ingramcontent.com/pod-product-compliance
Lightning Source LLC
Chambersburg PA
CBHW070121110526
44587CB00018BA/3349